How to Not Suck as a Manager

Five Facts to Bring Any Boss out of the Basement

AP Grow

DEDICATION

For managers everywhere. May you strive for the best of decency and professionalism in your efforts to move your organizations forward.

CONTENTS

ACKNOWLEDGMENTS

The author wishes to thank everyone who shared their experiences for this research. The collation of experiences, frustrations, and insights form the foundation of this book. Also, many thanks to Bob Lieter, Ms. Johnnie, Bud Smith, Wally Larson, Ken Austin, Paula Jean, and Coach Katherin Scott. Their great examples and counsel have inspired me to help all managers become better managers in the workplace.

FORWARD

Not long ago I was working with a national training account which my company held. The contract was to provide a series of seminars in a number of cities across the Western United States. The seminars were one-day classes in communication skills; an important set of skills everyone could use. One section of this seminar had to do with people who were more of a challenge. Almost every time my friends in the seminar world and I would present on this topic, at least one hand would go up to ask the question, "What do you do when the problem person is the boss?"

When this question would come up, as it usually did, I would reply with a question to the entire audience, "Show of hands, how many in here have ever worked with a bad boss?" Inevitably, in every city, hands would go up across the entire room. Hands would go up and the place would come alive with, "Oh yes, you *know* I've had a bad manager... I've had two." Sometimes I'd hear people tell me they've been through three! Usually, I would take a few moments to let people in the room briefly share some of their experiences.

It is amazing to me how energized, animated, and emotional people get as they share experiences about how badly they've been treated by bad supervisors. I had to agree. The experiences they would share were incredible. At first, I found it entertaining. Actually the whole room usually did. It was a good energy release. But when a person would speak of a current boss who was a bad boss, the room would get a bit somber. It was hitting too close to home.

The really alarming thing to me was how common the phenomena was. In city after city the stories would be there. Bad bosses everywhere, and not just a small number of them, but seemingly a significant percentage of the workforce. I was surprised by this so I decided to dust of my research skills and look more closely into the matter. This brought me to my first 'aha' moment. The first thing that I learned made me realize that I shouldn't have been surprised about the number of managers who suck in the workplace.

One of the reasons so many people have negative experiences with managers who suck is that far more than half of all managers out there have never had a single day of management training before assuming their supervisory role. Many, according to this same body of research, do not pursue, or even have the chance to pursue, any formal academic training in the area. This is true even after assuming management responsibilities. In many cases, they'll have a one to three day seminar on the subject and that's it.

Being a provider of professional and organizational development training, I'm not going to negate the value of any learning. I think though, that common sense would suggest that if the only instruction anyone gets on any topic is a sum total of one to three days, how much information is a person going to have to do their work well? Sadly, experience also tells us that even people with an MBA may suck as a manager.

Now let me ask another question. When things don't go quite right, when challenges arise, what do people rely on when they don't have the right maturity level, training, or discipline to guide them through what they are experiencing? Most counselors will tell you that without appropriate training, discipline, or maturity, people will rely on what comes naturally to them. Usually, this means defaulting to behaviors that they've developed over the course of their lives – often what they saw growing up. The point is, when it comes to managers, and their dealing with pressure situations at the office, their behavior is typically *not* based in good managerial practice; hence, again, a lot of bad managers.

I spoke with my associates about this, others like me, who were on the road regularly conducting similar seminars. I found that they were also experiencing similar reactions from groups they were working with. Time and again, in city after city, people would reveal bad manager stories. After a few months of hearing people relay their bad manager stories, I wondered if there were any behavioral patterns to these managers who sucked so badly. I reasoned that if I could find a number of common behaviors among managers who sucked, then I would know what to focus on in the seminars we provided to improve management productivity.

So I did what any enterprising individual would do in these modern times, I created a Web site. The URL for the site: www.howtonotsuckasamanager.com. Obviously I wasn't setting the bar too high here. I just wanted to find if there were common behaviors among bad managers. The easiest way to do that, it seemed, was to ask all of the people I spoke to, if they had a sucky manager story, to share it, in an anonymous way, on the Web site. Over 1200 experiences were submitted to the Web site. Even after a few hundreds contributions to the site, several focus areas began to emerge.

I have no grand illusions about being able to change all the bad managers of the world into good ones. But I will, at the very least, provide here a list of the behaviors that workers identified as the most common behaviors associated with bad managers. I will also provide strategies that supervisors can implement to bring anyone up from the ranks of sucky to being, at the very least, okay in their supervisor roll. Again, not looking for super manager status - just want managers to not suck.

Even before this book was finished I was already receiving feedback, not particularly flattering feedback, about the concept of this book. "Shouldn't people want to be good managers?" they would say. Sure, but there are already many books on that topic out there. What I haven't seen is any book that addresses bad management practices and provides fixes for them. For most people who have to endure a bad manager, I believe they'll be happy just to have that manager go from bad to okay. Excellence in management practice is something that can be addressed at a later time.

In this book I'm going to assume that it is you, the reader, who doesn't want to suck as a manager. So my directions will be to you, addressing people here in first person. I get full well though that there are many bad managers who may have no interest in purchasing this book. But those who report to these managers would love for them to receive this knowledge. If the learning is for someone else, just pass the knowledge along however you please. If this book ends up becoming the most popular anonymous gift on the planet so be it. If this is the situation for you, know that I'm not talking to you directly, but to the one you hope to help with this information. Now let's get to it.

FACT 1: MANAGERS WHO TREAT TEAM MEMBERS AS PEOPLE DON'T SUCK

I honestly don't know why I even bother anymore. For over three years I've been on time, done my work well, gotten projects done on time and under budget and the only thing I ever get from my boss 'Tom' is, well, silence. Maybe I should be grateful. Teammates who aren't up to par get ridden hard. Just once though, it would be nice to hear 'good job.' Just once.

Pam / Chicago

I'm going to put the bottom line up front for this one. The one thing employees want more than anything else; the one thing that will make the most difference as to their satisfaction in the workplace and their judgment about whether or not you suck as a manager is the degree to which you give your team members basic human consideration. Treat your team members as people and you stand a shot at not sucking as a manager. Forget or ignore this fact and you are bound to stay in suckville forever.

There's a world of difference between people and personnel. Personnel is the office that manages the human resource affairs of an organization. People are those that work in the organization. The success of your team lies entirely on the ability of your people to work together to get things done. To do that, you and your team members need a good working relationship. This requires that you treat your team members as people and not as mechanistic, emotionless automatons who exist only to do your bidding. How do you do this? Consider the following illustration.

When things aren't going quite as smooth as you might like; when an otherwise productive employee starts being less productive than normal, before going into spaz-out mode, first have a simple conversation with the team member. "Ron," you say, "I've noticed that during the past couple of days you've seemed a bit out of step. You don't have to share, if you don't want, but I'm concerned. Is everything okay?"

Now before you go all "That's not me, no way will I ever do that," hear me out. I'm not saying, you're going to play counselor here. Nor am I saying you need to be their friend, join hands, and sing, "We Are the World" around the campfire. What I am saying is that to not suck as a manager you need to be considerate of those you oversee. Sometimes this consideration even needs to be (gasp) on a personal level. Friendly. Professional. Considerate. Is this too much to ask? I hope not.

Let me say it a different way. Make sure that the people who report to you know that you care about them as people. How do you make sure they know this? Interact with them on a human level. You do this from a position of genuine interest. Feigning interest will not get the job done here. People aren't stupid. Folks can sense insincerity.

Now I know full well that when managers read this, there are some who will immediately think something like, "I don't give a rip if they like me or not. I need them to do what I tell them to and that's all. Management is not a popularity contest."

I have two replies to this. First, please read again, dear manager. I didn't say you need to like them or that they need to like you. What I am saying is, in order to not suck as a manager, team members need to know that *you* know who they are and that you have at least a basic consideration for them as fellow human beings. Say "Good job" when you see a good job. Say "Thank you" even if it is for standard work that happens every day.

Ask "Is there anything I can do to help?" even if you know there's not.

My experience is, and yours should be also, that as you demonstrate genuine care for your team members, as you learn about them on a personal level, you will find that they start showing a care for you too. This is not a bad thing to have happen, is it? Remember the primary goal is to have and show consideration for your team members. To do this you need to develop a good rapport with them.

Why is rapport so important?

It's true that people come to work for the paycheck. Sure they may love their job, but stop providing a paycheck for the work and see how long they continue to show up. This paycheck helps take care of physical needs, food, shelter, etc.; the most basic items on Maslow's hierarchy of needs. Now it's time for a pop quiz. After physical needs are taken care of, what comes next on Maslow's hierarchy? Social/emotional needs - that's right. People come to work because the need a pay check. People will stay with a job because they feel part of a team. We all need our physical needs taken care of and we also all need validation. Give this, and you add a critical element to people's well-being. Withhold this, and you lose the influence that would otherwise be available to you.

Again, I can imagine some managers saying. "My team members don't need me to build them up. I REALLY don't care if they like me. I really, truly, don't care. As long as the work gets done, that's the important thing."

This type of thinking leads me to the second reason consideration is the very first behavior managers who don't want to suck must master.

Turn the tables a moment. Who would you rather work for; someone you know and respect, or someone you don't know, or don't respect? Sure, work being what it is, you'll do the work in either case. But that's not the question. The question is who would you *rather* work for?

Most people will work harder for someone they know and respect. Managers who don't suck know this and conduct themselves accordingly. You know that respect is not automatically granted simply by virtue of a person's position. Your position as a manager gives you what is known as positional authority. With positional authority there's absolutely no automatic bestowal of loyalty or dedication. These things do not come with the role, they have to be earned. You earn this by putting time in with people on topics beyond the immediate work needs. Which brings us back to the topic of this chapter – consideration. Be sure your team members know that *you* know what being considerate means and that you are working with your team members as people.

This matter of basic human consideration is so foundationally important it has to be covered first. If your team members trust, care about, or respect you (and I mean respect stemming from having a good opinion of, not one bred of fear, or simply because of position) you have a hope of not only not sucking as a manager, but, in fact, being a good manager. If you don't have this, your success will be limited.

> *Our manager Alice didn't come to work today and let me tell you the whole place couldn't be happier. Here I am right now just surfing the internet. Others are enjoying soft drinks at their desk (a definite no no) and still others are talking to friends on their cell phones (another thing that's not supposed to happen at work). None of us care. Why? Because Alice doesn't care - at least not about us. She cares if she looks good. She cares if her reports are turned in on time, but if any of us has something come up while working to accomplish this, too bad for us. So screw it. Today, we play. If we're lucky, she'll be out tomorrow too and we'll play some more!*

> *Macy / Ft. Collins*

Do you really think employees will care about the work, let alone you, if you don't have a genuine care for them? Caring matters. It matters more than most managers realize. Managers who suck don't even care that caring matters. That's why they suck. Here's how to not to suck at treating your team members as people.

Talk to Your Team Members

Talk to your team members. Talk to your team members not just when issues arise, but well before they do, and regularly. They need to know, before a crisis occurs, that you know about them. Ask questions. For example, "Hey, Marge, you mentioned your son Mark is into martial arts now. How's that going?" or "Hey, John, how was your weekend?" Simple questions, but asked regularly, with genuine interest can make the difference between having a team that cares about what you have to say, and one that couldn't care less. I'm not saying this first characteristic is the 'end all be all' for managers. What I am saying is if you want people to do well at work, they need to know they're doing it for someone who knows them and values their work.

If you've never before had honest, personal-level conversations with your team members, you're going to get some strange looks, perhaps even some jokes. There will likely be suspicion as well. Some team members may not be too interested or comfortable with your efforts. That's okay. Keep it simple. Don't let this dissuade you. Just roll with it. You know what you're doing. Tell your team members you feel its time you get to know them better. You believe it will help you become better able to help them in their work – which, of course, is true. As time goes on, most will appreciate the gesture. Again, they may be surprised, but if you stay true to your plan, they'll come around.

One other point to add here; As you ask questions of your team members, and maybe share a little about yourself, be sure you do more listening than speaking. This is not a time to one up your employees or dominate conversation. Pay attention to their interests. Take notes. Care more for them than for yourself. This is not a bad piece of advice for all relations, right?

Give Consideration

When issues arise, ask about the issue first. Never jump to conclusions or assume anything. If a person is distracted by personal matters, consider asking the rest of the team members if they'd be okay if the person took the rest of the day off to take care of matters at home, with pay of course. Don't let yourself be taken advantage of with this idea, but every once in a while, as needed, this would probably go along way with your team members. This is one way to improve in the humanity department. It is always a good idea to also know what counseling resources your organization has available. Refer your team members to the appropriate resources if you feel this will help. How many more can you think of? Better still, how many more will you implement?

Compliment

I can't tell you the number of experiences collected in our research that has this as its theme. People, regardless of how old they are, where they're from, their sex, or any other demographic you care to mention – everyone wants to be acknowledged for their contributions. Recognition - it's what I call a human universal. People want, and to a degree even need, to know that others care about them and that their effort in the workplace is appreciated.

Yes, I know every employee is getting paid to be at work. A sucky manager will think, maybe even say, "Your pay is your thanks. That is your show of appreciation." As we all know, and as was said before, people work because they need to. They stay because the want to. Does this mean that you can't show some mindfulness towards the people who report to you? Of course not.

Good managers keep in mind how team members will react personally to things and act accordingly. Would a team member be glad to hear some praise given about them to other people? Probably so. Would they appreciate every now and then a simple, "Thanks for taking care of that so well" Again, probably so. Would they be happy to see their manager take credit for something *they* did? Definately not. The more you can do to foster genuine, healthy, human relations among team members, the more you will keep yourself out of suckland and into the realm of sound managerial practice.

The Suckometer and Working with People

Behaviors:

- Telling employees what to think, feel, and say
- No care for the personal welfare of team members
- No concern about non-work matters of any kind
Suckomoter Reading: 100% suck

Behaviors:

- Asks about welfare of others but doesn't really care
- Knows employees have children but not names
- Shares a little about self but only superficially
Suckometer Reading: not bad, not great, 50% suck

Behaviors:

- Cares about employees. Asks how things are going and listens when they discuss family topics or other matters of interest to them
- Notices when team members seem a bit 'off' and asks if anything can be done to help.

- Interacts with team members as fellow human beings.

Suckometer Reading: 0% suck. A manager who understands how to work with people!

Self Check

Where do you see yourself on the Suckometer for consideration of people? Rate yourself on a scale of 0 to 10. 0 is you could give a seminar on the topic. 10 is no way should you be a manager. (High scores on a Suckometer – not good.)

Sockometer Self-Assessment for Consideration of People:

_____

Action Plan

Regardless of your self-assessment score, consider ways to improve in this skill and put these ideas into practice. Use the following space to write your action plans for improving skills in consideration for people.

_____

_____

_____

_____

_____

FACT 2: MANAGERS WHO HAVE AWARENESS AT MULTIPLE LEVELS DON'T SUCK

Our boss is so (censored word) clueless. Three times over the last three months I reminded him that executives from the regional office were going to visit our office in September. What does he do? He schedules himself out for that week. He buys non-refundable tickets to Florida for him and his girlfriend. "Oh, sorry," he says, "You'll need to take care of hosting them." (Not a request.) What an idiot. I know that he's just playing dumb because he is majorly uncomfortable with real leaders. I suspect, though, that he is clueless about how to do his own job. Either that or he has no interest in helping team members with their work. Which is also sad.

Manuel / San Jose

Being aware of things beyond their team is another area that managers who don't want to suck must tend to. Be aware of team members' needs, the team's position in the organization, and the organization's situation compared with organizations in the profession. Managers who have it, don't suck, managers who don't have it, do suck. Many people shared experiences with us which makes this point clear.

If you don't want to suck as a manager, you need to be aware of what's going on around you. You have to know what's happening with team members in order to know how to be most helpful to them. After all, isn't that what a manager is for, to help remove roadblocks? In my opinion, this is exactly what your first priority should be; to remove roadblocks for your team members, certainly not create them.

> *I recently left a job which I loved because my manager, Mr. B, was totally clueless about who was doing what on our team. I was in charge of account receivables. Others were in charge of payroll and filing. What did I find myself doing more of? Not only my work but my coworker's too. Why was this? Because others on the team simply weren't getting the job done. If the job doesn't get done, then our team looks bad. If our performance is bad, we can get replaced by a third-party firm that could do what we do.*

I've heard upper management mention this more than once. So even though it's not in my job, I find myself doing the work. I do this because I don't happen to want to lose my job.

Whenever I would speak to Mr. B about it, he never cared. He was more concerned about what we wore to work than the work others on my team were not doing. A few weeks ago, even though payroll was dangerously close to not meeting the week's deadline, the only thing Mr. B brought up in the team meeting was the need to wear appropriate shoes to work. Shoes !! are you kidding me? Our team could've been months maybe weeks away from being axed and all he cared about were shoes! That was the day I realized no amount of pointing things out to him and no amount of me carrying other people's work was going to keep the inevitable from happening. I started looking for a new job that night. Even though the job is farther away, it's worth it. Everyone knows their job and takes their responsibilities seriously. Life is so much better when everyone is doing their part. Not coincidently, within four months after my leaving, the whole payroll team, including Mr. B was let go and the service was outsourced.

Jane / New Orleans

Again, this is only one of hundreds of experiences people shared, but the theme is always the same; a manager should know what to focus on, but doesn't. Nor does a sucky manager seem willing to change their focus even when it's pointed out to them. Perhaps the greater flaw is an unwillingness to listen and learn. Suckville indeed.

There are three levels of awareness. Good managers have at least a couple of these traits. Great managers will be aware at all three of these levels. Managers who suck don't have a clue about what's going on in any of these areas.

Three Levels of Awareness

The first level of awareness is team-level awareness. If you don't want to suck in the area of awareness you need to be aware of what your team's primary responsibilities are and how well each member of the team is meeting these responsibilities. Higher level supervisors usually assume that a manager knows the work of the team. If the manager comes from the ranks of the team itself, then there's a decent chance the higher level supervisor's assumption is correct. Unfortunately, this is not always the case. Actually, this is often not the case at all.

Managers can come from all different areas of an operation. If you are a manager who has been put in charge of a team you didn't come out of, then you owe it to those you supervise to get to know each one of the team members (see Fact 1) and also become familiar with the work they are responsible for. Job shadow for a while. Maybe take a course in the area they are responsible for. Talk to the previous team leader if possible. Know the roadblocks they may have. Know how to help remove those roadblocks and, most importantly, take action to remove those blocks so the team member can be most productive. This is the first level of awareness you need to have to not suck in the area of awareness.

Unfortunately, many managers don't know who is doing what on their team. Or worse, they know someone isn't carrying their weight but they choose not to do anything about it. We'll get to how to deal with that later.

Knowing what is happening on your team is the first level of awareness. There are two other levels of awareness that a manager who doesn't want to suck should know about. The way I see it, if you don't want to suck you should try for something more. In fact, aspire to being good at what you do. In the area of awareness you need to not only be aware of what's happening on your team and make adjustments as necessary, but also be aware of the roll your team is playing in the organization and be looking for ways to contribute more.

The more a team contributes in an organization, the more valuable a team becomes to the organization. Good managers know this. Sucky managers – this never even occurs to them.

The third level of awareness a manager can have is knowing where their organization is relative to the entire industry. I know this is generally the domain of VPs and CEOs, but I believe managers who want to excel will have this on their radar as well. Why? Because being informed about where ones organization is relative to the industry can help a manager be a more effective manager. How is this possible? Let me give you an example.

For decades, many U.S. based companies have been moving the production-side of their operations to overseas locations. When sports equipment manufacturer, K2 Sports, decided to do this, it sent shockwaves through the small town they were in on Vashon Island, a small island in the Puget Sound, not far from Seattle, Washington. They announced that they were going to move much of the production to an overseas facility.

As mentioned earlier, companies moving their production work overseas is not a new thing so in my humble opinion, it should have been no surprise when K2 Sports announced this. What did surprise me was the amount of press this announcement received –

particularly about how this move would impact the local economy, as well as the surprise to the local community.

Here's my point. I know it's the CEO's job to look out for the welfare of a company. It's a manager's job, at least in part, to look out for the welfare of his or her team members. At a team level, shouldn't a manager be aware of how to help his or her team members too? Sucky managers don't even know what their own team members are doing. Okay managers will at least know this. Good managers will look for more ways their team can contribute to an organization. Even better managers will be aware of what's happening, not only in their organization, but also what's happening in the industry. As I said earlier, this is what I call field awareness. From day one of his or her hire, good managers learn their field and do what they can to help others adjust to the field as well.

Now, I don't know the particulars of the situation for K2, but I'll toss out some ideas for any manager who wants not only to not suck, but to be seen as good manager. If employees have an education benefit, managers can recommend team members take advantage of that. Anything that can be done to help team members improve themselves is always a good thing. Managers can also encourage team members to take on new and different responsibilities. Stretching to become more versatile job-wise is always a good thing. Even if the particular production-related job can't continue, more transferable skills, like management, or quality assurance work, can continue at another place. Again, giving team members as many opportunities as possible to improve their own skill set will help them and the manager too. Losing a team member to a different team will change the original team but it's likely to be better for the individual.

But I digress. Remember the current topic here is not sucking as a manager by being aware. Aware of what individuals are doing on the team, and what they may need, aware of what the team's role is relative to the company and how that can be improved, and, at the highest level, awareness of the organization relative to the entire field. At each level, making whatever adjustments are possible to keep things moving ahead.

How to Not Suck at Awareness

Team Level Awareness

At the team level, managers who don't want to suck in the area of awareness will spend time with team members. They will know the problems team members have and help resolve them. Managers who do not suck remove roadblocks, not create them. Creating roadblocks is the handywork of managers who suck.

Organizational Level Awareness

At the organizational level, managers who don't want to suck will know what other teams in the organization are doing, or more importantly, what they are not doing. What other teams are not doing or what they can be doing better is what provides an opening for the aware team manager. Please don't misunderstand. I am not suggesting any manager look to for ways to undermine or otherwise subvert the work of other teams. I *am* suggesting that managers who don't suck see opportunities for their own team members to do more and lead their teams in doing just that. The more you can do this for your team, the better off your team and the organization will be.

Field Level Awareness

At the field level, as I've already said, managers should know what's going on in the world, speak about this with their team members, and do what they can to help their team members stay on top of their own game. Though it's true people are responsible for their own path, and CEOs are responsible for a company's path, this doesn't mean that a manager can't help in both categories.

So stay tuned into what's happening in the world. What are the major companies in your field doing? What are the major individual players up to? What about suppliers for your company? Or the political conditions or economics in countries that may supply these resources? All of these things, and so many more, can impact an industry. The more you know, the more you can do.

The Suckometer and Awareness

Behaviors

- No clue what team members are doing, or care
- No care for the organization, only for oneself
- No ability to help team members
- Does not share information with team

Suckometer Reading: 100% suck

Behaviors:

- Some knowledge of what team members do
- Knowledge of what the organization is up to but only as it concerns the sucky manager
- Catches only the headlines of world news. Nice that they know at least this much, but still not nearly as much as what a good manager should know

Suckometer Reading: not bad, not great; 50% suck

Behaviors

- Has knowledge of what team members are doing and helps whenever possible. Has situational awareness. Removes roadblocks.
- Knows what is happening in the organization and how the team can be help the organization.
- Keeps an eye on what is happening in the world with respect to the profession.

Suckometer Reading: 0% suck. A fully aware manager!

Self Check

Where do you see yourself on the Suckometer for awareness? Rate yourself on a scale of 0 to 10. 0 is you could give a seminar on the topic. 10 is no way should you be a manager. (High scores on a Suckometer – not good.)

Suckometer Self-Assessment for Awareness: _____

Action Plan

Regardless of your self-assessment score, consider ways to improve in this skill and put these ideas into practice. Use the following space to write your action plans for improving skills in awarness?

_____

_____

_____

_____

FACT 3: MANAGERS WHO KNOW HOW TO PRACTICE REAL DELAGATION DON'T SUCK

Managers probably come with all kinds of issues, but the issues that lead them to being a micromanager is one I can't figure out. Was it not enough control as a child? Maybe siblings who constantly said they would never amount to anything? Maybe good old fashioned power-tripping. He has more concern for being in control than developing his team members by assigning anything new or innovating to them. Sad. Annoying too, but mostly sad. I've known Mark for many years so this is no surprise. I roll with it but others don't. This probably explains the amount of turnover on this team but he'll never see it.

Sam / Eugene

The third behavior on the list of how to not suck as a manager is to not be a micromanager. Or in other words, practice real delegation. Whenever I give this presentation to a live audience I always start out by asking, "How many here have ever been managed by a micromanager?" Typically, I'll see hands raised from at least 75% of the people in the room. It's amazing. Invariably, the hands raised will be accompanied with audible comments like, "Oh you KNOW, I've been there." Others will say, "Sometimes I think I work in micromanager land." Then someone else will say, "Work there? I have a permanent address there" Yes…. I think I can hear them even now.

I'm not going to go into why micromanaging may be so wide-spread. I have my guesses, relatively little management training by people in management positions, managers with low self-confidence, managers with control issues, maybe a fear of letting other people do well and getting all the credit; who knows? I wonder, does it even really manner? Probably not. All you need to know, if you're someone who falls into this category, you need to stop this or you will forever be considered a manager who sucks.

The more important thing to do is raise awareness about this behavior, come to an agreement that it's not a good thing, and share strategies on how to correct it. So here we go.

First a definition: Micromanaging is overseeing things to the point that the one who was told they are responsible for the work feels little or no real control over it.

Once again:

Micromanaging is overseeing things to the point that the one who is told they were responsible for the work feels little or no real control over it.

To borrow the stylings of comedian Jeff Foxworthy, here are signs you may be a micromanager.

If you find yourself asking for updates from your subordinates way more than is necessary for the job... you might be a micromanager.

If you find yourself giving 'advice' or 'guidance' often and without it being asked for... you might be a micromanager.

If you find yourself giving 'advice' or 'guidance' when it's not needed... you might be a micromanager.

If you find yourself insisting on your own way even after you've 'delegated' the work...you might be a micromanager.

If you think maybe you should take back some of the work assigned out because you, and only you, don't like the direction things are going… you might be a micromanager.

If you believe no one on your team is as good at the work as you… you might be a micromanager.

If people on your team have said you are a person who likes to micromanage… you probably are a micromanager.

I don't think I need to elaborate on the definition too much more here. I think most would agree, you know it when you see it. You certainly know it when you're experiencing it. The problem is the managers who do it, usually don't recognize what they are doing, and even when it is pointed out to them, they aren't interested in changing. Thus a sucky manager moniker. I get that it can be difficult to change this. I understand it can be tough to release control when the ultimate responsibility belongs to you, the manager. Still learning how to let go in this regard is crucial to success. What are the effects of micromanaging?

> *Unbelievable. I have no other words for it. Completely unbelievable. I wish I had other words for it. I wish there were other words for it, but there's not. I cannot believe what I have to deal with, or that I stay around to deal with it. Resumes are everywhere.*

Hopefully something will come up soon. What really sucks? Being paid to do a job and not being allowed to do it. 'Sara' thinks she can do it better. This has got to be the most frustrating, demeaning, disrespectful, unprofessional and just plain annoying thing I've ever experienced. And yes, it really sucks! If she's not taking the work completely off my desk, she's riding my behind so hard with questions and 'advice' about the projects she has left with me that there is no way I can focus on the work.

Mike / Seattle

If you've experienced it, and by my frequent informal surveys I'm confident most people have, you know exactly what the effects are.

Frustrating. Not too many things rank higher on the frustration list than having responsibility for something and not being allowed to actually take responsibility for it. It's like, "Hey, why don't you go ahead and be in charge of this project... oh, just kidding.. haha!" Not funny, but that's how it goes, and that's how it feels when being micromanaged.

A feeling of no confidence. Micromanaged employees feel the micromanaging manager has no confidence in them. If there was confidence, the sucky manager wouldn't be bugging them so often about the project, now would they? So it goes. Minds spin, workers question. Work doesn't get done.

Belittled, Disrespected. Nothing says 'you can't handle this' quite like not being left alone to do the work.

In short, pretty much every feeling a good manager should not want to leave with an employee, this is what micromanaging does. So why does it happen?

A manager who micromanagers may not realize the impact their behavior is having. Sadly, they may not even care. Most sources agree though, trust and a structured approach for handing off the work, are core ingredients for overcoming micromanaging behavior. If you don't want to suck, trust that people on the team can do what they're being asked to do. Trust that they'll ask questions if they have them. Trust that they'll make things happen on time and under budget and, most especially, trust that things will be okay even if the work is not done the way you would do it. This is where trust comes into play. Now let's get into to a structured approach for practicing real delegation.

I love the way former President Reagan put it when asked about the success of his time in the President's office. Political party loyalty aside, I think most people would agree he had a pretty successful time in office;

overseeing a strong economy, national crime rates down, and ushering in the end of the cold war, even to the point of seeing the Berlin wall come down.

When asked about this, President Reagan was his regular humble self as he gave what I consider to be a very insightful reply. He said essentially – paraphrasing here, 'yes we had a good run it, but it wasn't all me. I had certain things I wanted to get done while in office and I knew there was no way I could get it all done on my own, so I put good people in charge, and stayed out of their way." I think that pretty well sums up what good managers do in the delegation area; they put good people in charge and get out of their way.

Bad managers will reply, "Well I don't have any good people to work with." To which I reply, "Whose responsibility is it to help them improve?" and "What do you think you can do to help them improve?" Of course the answer to these two questions are the manager. One definite thing a manager can do to help team members improve is broaden their skill set by giving them new tasks to do and helping them become proficient in these new skills. This is the heart of delegation, and remember the reason we're on this topic is because real delegation will eliminate micromanaging – the two cannot exist at the same time, they are mutually exclusive.

Remember also the foundation for real delegation is trust. The amount of trust you yourself would want from your boss needs to be the amount of trust you should be ready to give your team members. With trust as the foundation, here are the three steps to real delegation.

Step 1: Provide clear details about the work. Providing clear detail includes all functions, facets, possible pitfalls, the scope of what needs to be done, and the timeline for completing it.

I often find that poor managers have poor communication skills. Quality delegation, on the other hand, requires quality communication. Quality communication is communication that leaves no doubt as to what a project entails. This is provided in multiple ways. Speaking about the work that needs done is, of course, the first step. Allow the team member time to ask questions. The level and type of questions should indicate whether or not there is a clear and correct view of the work to be done. But just to be sure, if the work situation warrants it, you have the team member follow up this conversation with an email message which summarizes what was said and what their plans are for accomplishing this. Demonstrate, explicate, have your team member share their view of the work - whatever you feel you need to do to be sure you have conveyed the clearest picture possible, and more importantly, to ensure you have verification that *they* have the same picture in mind as you do. A basic tenet of communication is that the sender is responsible for ensuring a message understood as intended. If a message is not correctly, or fully understood, it is not the receiver but the sender of the message who must be held accountable for this. Never assume a team member knows exactly what you mean.

Step 2: Provide a regular update schedule. Determine together what the frequency of updates should be through the duration of the project. If the work has some degree of freedom as to completion date, then let the team member take some time to create what he or she feels is an appropriate timeline for the task. With a clear picture of the project in mind a team member should have all the information they need to set up a timeline for the task. I am not saying, have them go off to create a timeline and then meet with them to completely undue the work they did. What I am saying is work together on the timeline to determine a reasonable schedule.

After the project timeline is determined together, establish a regular update schedule to go from the start of the work through to the end of it. Depending on the nature of the work this may be a weekly, bi-weekly, or perhaps monthly meeting. Most people work more effectively when they must be accountable for their work.

Together create the update schedule to help your team member stay consistently working towards the goal of a completed project. This will help you keep your peace of mind by knowing when you will receive progress reports about the work. You, dear manager who doesn't want to suck, do not mess with this schedule by regular unsolicited (and probably unwanted) drop-ins or fly-bys. Leave it to the team member to decide if more updates are needed beyond the scheduled dates. This brings us to step three in a structured delegation process.

Step 3: Keep Your Door Open. Make sure the team member knows that at any time they need or want, they can come to you for advice, counsel or questions. This too has a duel benefit. The team member has the safety net of a manager who is ready to provide help at any time and you, as the manager, continue to affirm your role as mentor, supervisor, and leader of your team. When the team member does come to you for input, welcome the visit. They are following the system you've put in place. Never make an employee sorry for approaching you.

Related to this, never make an employee sorry for coming to you with questions or concerns of any type. Even if, or rather *particularly if,* it happens to be information about you or something about your team that you may not want to hear. If an employee has courage enough to do this, you need to respect this and be glad for this. I cannot tell you the number of experiences I have heard personally or read about where employees have tried to share information that would be valuable for a manager to know only to have the manager get upset at the team member when they heard the information.

Managers who won't hear unpleasant information, without a cost to the message bearer, are managers that suck. We're wanting to raise the bar higher for all managers here, so listen up. I'm looking to help managers who suck, not to suck quite so much. At the same time, I'm hoping to help managers who aren't bad, do even better. So for both groups, here's a tip. Whenever information comes your way that you may not want to hear, think on this - whatever is being said, you would rather know than not know. Knowledge is a good thing. Refer to Fact 2 for a reminder of why this is so. When you get information you'd rather not hear, welcome it, thank the messenger and move forward with a better knowledge of your situation, whatever that situation is.

The digression from the point is worth the detour. The point here is to not suck as a manager, you need to not be a micromanager. Micromanaging is bad. Nurturing team members, and trusting them with assigned work through genuine, authentic delegation ... good. If you want to not suck as a manager you need to not be a micromanager and get good at delegation.

The Suckometer and Real Delegation

Behaviors:

- Manager puts value of own ideas over others
- Unwilling to consider input from others as potentially equal or (dare we say it) even more insightful and useful
- Frequent unsolicited giving of 'advice' or 'guidance'
- Saying " I only want them to do things, right". Translation: The sucky managers way
  Suckometer Reading: 100% suck

Behaviors:

- Seeks updates sometimes outside of the agreed upon schedule
- Has some do special work but only a select few
  Suckometer Reading: not bad, not great. 50% suck

Behaviors

- Gives growth opportunities to all team members
- Guides team members with mutually agreed upon expectations, schedules, and check-in times
- Openly praises the talents of team members. where talents need developing, manager actively mentors
  Suckometer Reading: 0% suck . A real delegator !

Self Check

Where do you see yourself on the Suckometer for delegation? Rate yourself on a scale of 0 to 10. 0 is you could give a seminar on the topic. 10 is no way should you be a manager. (High scores on a Suckometer – not good.)

Suckometer Self-Assessment for Real Delegation: _____

Action Plan

Regardless of your self-assessment score, consider ways to improve in this skill and put these ideas into practice. Use the following space to write your action plans for improving skills in real delegation.

_____
_____
_____
_____
_____
_____

FACT 4: MANAGERS WHO TAKE ACTION TO STOP NON-TEAM PLAYER BEHAVIORS DON'T SUCK

Three jobs. Three jobs I have worked where an otherwise good work group is messed up by one idiot and a manager won't kick him or her to the curb. In order of experiences: It's been a pervert, a wino, and a lazy bum on my teams. Why could they NOT be let go? This too varied by place. The pervert was a member of the family-owned business. The wino, 'just misunderstood' and the lazy one was 'really good with error-free reports.' As if no one but her could write error-free reports.

Every one of these jobs were with good companies, good benefits, and all close to home but each one had me wanting to run because just one person was allowed to do whatever the heck they wanted with no regard for any other person on the team. Each one of these times would have been fine. All had great people to work with but one. But that one person, in each job, every freaking time, made being there unbearable.

What on earth is a manager paid for if not to take care of the problems like these? Is it so hard? Is it so very hard to do? It must be because no manager I've had seems able to handle this simple thing.

Karen / Dallas

Without a doubt, not taking action to stop non-team player behaviors will create anger among other team members faster than anything else. If you've ever been on a team supervised by a manager who does this, or rather doesn't do this, you know exactly what I mean here. One of the absolute suckiest traits of a sucky manager, according to all who submitted experiences along these lines, is to not take action with a team member who is not being a team player.

Of course, all five facts discussed in this book are important for success as a manager, but this one topic, is so big that it requires its own separate training. Not long ago I dedicated an audio seminar to this matter. Its title: Change or Go: How to Stop Non-Team Player Behavior in the Workplace. Here, I'll go over the highlights of that work, but just so you know, more detailed materials are available. Yup, shameless self-promotion. I went there.

If I asked one thousand employees to choose three of the most aggravating behaviors a sucky manager could display, my experience tells me that this one would make the list for at least 900 of them. Why is this? Because few things annoy people faster than working hard doing what is needed while at the same time having a teammate not pulling his or her weight, or worse, fighting against team cohesion and productivity.

These feelings are not hard to understand. What's hard to understand is how non-team player behaviors are allowed by so many managers for so long.

"So I let someone get away with some things. What's the harm?" The sucky manager asks. The most illustrative examples I can come up with are often sports related. This one is no exception. Is there any coach, of any professional sports team, in any country, who would allow a team member to take the ball and run that ball in the direction of the opposing team's goal? I'm thinking no. It happens once, okay, a mistake. Have a seat on the bench, think about it. It happens again? The coach starts thinking 'maybe I don't have the right person for my team here.' (And the fans would agree.) A third time? For a professional ball player, there probably won't be a third time. Yet figuratively speaking, sucky managers will let a non-team player run the ball the wrong way every day. Day after day, week after week, month after month, and all too often, year after year. It has to stop.

When I say non-team player behavior, I'm talking about any time a team member is running the wrong way with the ball; a person on the team who is not only not helping, but actually hindering the work. Non-team player behavior can slow down the progress of an otherwise productive team to almost a full stop. What do I mean by non-team player behavior? Let me give you a few examples; let's take them A to Z.

A-holes	Haters	Offenders	Victims
Bullies	Idiots	Pitypartiers	Wierdos
Crazies	Jokers	Quipmiesters	Xerox addicts
Dimwits	Killjoys	Ridiculers	Yellers
Egomaniacs	Lazies	Sarcastics	*and*
Favorites	Manics	Thieves	Zombies
Gossips	Negativists	Users	

It's like trying to paddle a canoe with a person who is not paddling, or worse, paddling the opposite direction. It causes frustration and hurt feelings. It lowers moral, and destroys camaraderie. Obviously, this has a negative impact on overall team performance. Managers who don't want to suck must address this. Here's what I recommend.

Wait. Sorry not ready to go there yet.

Before I get into a procedure for resolving non-team player behavior, we have to first ask why is not addressing it such a prevalent thing? I'm going to suggest one idea. No doubt this is not the only possibility, but it's the most common reason cited so I'll share it. Managers who do not address non-team player behavior seem, in general, to be managers who don't like confrontation. I know this because as I've counseled hundreds of managers over the years, these are the exact words they'll use.

"But I don't like confrontation." (In whiny voice.)

There may be other reasons. A non-team player may be a manager's favorite person making him or her untouchable. Maybe the employee's skill set is seen as so valuable that the manager justifies the team member's opposing behavior. I think in most cases though, it's simply a manager's discomfort of addressing the non-team player behavior that allows the behavior to persist.

To this I can only say, "Grow a spine!" One of the most important roles a manager has is to remove roadblocks so team members can be more productive. If someone on the team is being the roadblock, then the manager who doesn't want to suck will do something about it. Countless contributors to our research believe this is one of the most important tasks managers are paid to do.

By the way, many non-team players know that most people have a distaste for confrontation. This is what they rely on to continue to do what they are doing. As long as a sucky manager continues not to take action against non-team players, non-team player behavior will persist.

I don't want to go into too much detail here. Like I mentioned earlier, I have more detailed work on this topic. For our purposes here, all you need to know is that you must develop within yourself a willingness to deal with non-team player behavior issues. Having a plan in place should give you the foundation you need to act. There are many strategies out there for curbing non-team player behavior in the workplace. I'm going to describe a general approach that you should be able to adapt to meet your specific needs.

Team Agreement

Before you begin this process though, it is extremely, I'll say vitally important that you speak very candidly to your own manager and to your Human Resource officers about what you are doing and why *before* you start down this path. If you are starting this process only to help the team in general, that's great, no problem. If, on the other hand, you are doing this to help the team and with a specific person on your team, then let that be known too. Explain what is happening, explain what you are doing about it, and ask for their support. If you do not have their support, then you have a very different matter to deal with. We'll assume you have their support in these steps.

To not suck as a manager in the take action department, you have first got to make it clear what the expectations are for your team. I recommend involving the entire team in the creation of a written list of behaviors that team members want to see from each other.

It is also important to make a separate, well-understood, list of behaviors that are not ok, or in other words, the non-team player behaviors. This is an important first step because there is no way you can deal with non-team player behavior unless everyone on the team knows exactly what these behaviors are. Because you'll never be able to know beforehand all of the possible distractions to team productivity, the last item on your list of non-team player behaviors should probably read something like this, "Any behavior that distracts from the cohesion, effectiveness, or productivity of the team."

Who decides if a certain behavior is a non-team player behavior or not? You do, dear manager! What is non-team player behavior? You'll know it when you see it, and, if you don't want to suck as a manager, you'll act on it. The list of ok and not okay behaviors are the most basic items for the agreement. There are other items you can add such as the organization mission and vision, team purpose, and other related items. Do the behaviors first and you'll have a good start.

Before I go any further, I want to make it clear that wherever you work, there will be specific action steps for helping team members become better team players. What I'm sharing here are general steps that would help improve any situation. However, you must be aware of what the procedures are where you work and follow those steps.

Whatever your organization has in place must take precedence over the general list of steps you'll find presented here or anywhere else. Have a conversation with your own manager and the appropriate HR representatives before you start down this road. For your own professional protection, and for that of your team members', it is imperative that you follow your organization's procedures in this area. Again, I am sharing a general approach here. Adopt what you believe can help you succeed, as well as you can, within the guidelines of your own organization's policies.

Another footnote, the moment you start making it clear to everyone on the team what is not acceptable behavior, many non-team players will know things are going to change. Many non-team players know the HR policies better than their managers. This is why at the very least, a manager who doesn't want to suck has to be up on these policies as well. Leverage this knowledge to help the team and the whole organization move forward.

Initiating Your Team Agreement

After the list of acceptable and unacceptable behaviors is created, posted, and well known, the flagrant non-team players will know something's up. Actually, they will likely know something is up the moment you and other team members begin documenting what constitutes a desired team player and what is meant by unacceptable, non-team player behavior. You will know they know because non-team players will likely object, almost immediately, to what you are doing. They will object to "being controlled." They will defend notions that it should be okay to 'gossip a little' or arrive late "every so often". Be ready for this. Keep your replies polite, professional, and on point. "What do you mean by every so often? "How often would it be okay for a pro basketball player to take the ball in the wrong direction?" Non-team player behavior to any degree is not good. It isn't harmless, it isn't cute. If you don't want to suck as a manager, it will not be okay for team members to behave in ways that can harm team productivity.

The really cool part about this fact is that as you take action to stop non-team player behavior every other member of the team will appreciate this effort. You likely know from your own experience that in most cases there is only one member on the team who is not being a team player. The really amazing thing to me is how badly, if left unchecked, a non-team player can mess up an otherwise highly functional team. The moment you begin to say 'enough is enough,' you will find most of the rest of the team, the rest who want a fair, game-free, and more productive workplace, will rally to your side.

Practicing Your Team Agreement

After making it clear what the desired and unacceptable behaviors are, a manager who doesn't want to suck will call out the non-team player behavior when seen or heard. I want to emphasize, when seen or heard *by you*. Be cautious of second-hand reports. Second-hand reports are known in the judicial system as hearsay. Hearsay is not allowed in the courts for good reason. Game players can make things up and you don't want to be a toy in someone else's game. I'm not saying not to address the hearsay. You just need to address it in an informative manner rather than a take action manner. Something like, "I have heard from others…." for example. It should go without saying, but I will say it anyway, that you should never take action against a team member on hearsay. You need personal, first-hand evidence of non-team player behavior. To use anything else in your effort to improve your team dynamic, while well intentioned, is not wise. Your purpose in these cases is simply to let the alleged non-team player know what others are saying because he or she should want to know about it.

When you have witnessed the non-team player behavior, keep yourself on point about it. These conversations need to be as close to the occurrence as possible but always in private. Be professional, non-confrontational, and stick to the facts. It should go without saying that these things need to remain private matters between you and your team member. For this specific part of a manager's life, I highly recommend Crucial Conversations by Peterson.

It is a huge oversimplification to sum up the work of Peterson's team in just a sentence or two but if I had to do so, I would use words from their Vital Smarts website. "If you can't talk honestly with nearly anybody about almost anything, you can expect poor results." A fundamental tenet of the Crucial Conversations® work is that people (including managers) should have good relations with the people they are around so when a heart to heart conversation is needed, the personal trust, respect, and cache will be available to make potentially difficult conversations as productive as possible. Makes sense, right?

To review, Step 1: Identify the team behaviors that you expect to see, as well as those that are not okay, and list them in a document that I like to call a team agreement. Step 2: When you observe things that are not okay, you have a conversation with the team member about them. Keep the conversation as close to the incident as possible and always polite, professional, and private.

Sticking with Your Team Agreement

Moving into new material now. Step 3: The next time you hear or see behavior that is not consistent with the team agreement, you have another conversation but this time, the conversation is noted in writing and kept on file. Now again, you must follow your own organization's policies here. For every point in a change process you need to involve the assistance of your own manager and human resource people. Make very sure your own supervisor and the appropriate HR people are onboard and part of this process. Whatever the appropriate steps are according to your organization's policies, those are the steps you take.

Another repetition here. At this point you can expect some emotional feedback from non-team players. "Come on, what's wrong with a little picking fun at Tom's expense every now and then" or "Are you kidding me? You know I like to stir things up in these meetings. The meetings would be boring otherwise. It's just the way I am" or "It's not my fault I'm late sometimes. Can I help the traffic patterns?" Friends, you will hear a litany of responses when you take this next step, and every one of them, in my experience, boils down to one way or another of saying either 'It's not my fault' or 'It's not that bad'. The problem is, it is that bad, which is why it has to be dealt with.

For the good of the team, if you don't want to suck as a manager, you will take these steps. You will stay professional and on point as you speak with them, but for sure you must take action. In the end, they may or may not change, but that will be their decision, not yours, and for the good of the team and your organization, you will take the appropriate action.

At this point I think it's worth differentiating here, those who know they're playing games from those who don't. Some who are intentionally fighting against the team, and some who aren't aware they're behavior is way too disruptive to the team – they simply haven't received the appropriate counsel yet. They talk about personal things more than work, they gossip, maybe they're not dressing appropriately – whatever it is – it's not helping the team be as productive as they can be. With these folks, one conversation and it's done with. We'll go into one approach for these conversations in the section for Fact 5 so stay tuned for that.

The other group, those who are knowingly and willfully behaving in a way that is contrary to team goals, are the ones we are talking about here. First, you have documented the desired and unacceptable behavior. Next, as we just listed, you have had a conversation with them to ensure they know that what they are doing, or not doing, cannot continue any longer – maybe it was okay in the past, but in the interest of taking the team to the next level, it's not okay anymore. Next, you continue on the path prescribed by your manager and your HR team, until the non-team player either changes or chooses to go. More information is available on this topic in my other works with this time same title. Please pick up those sources if you want more information on the topic.

In my experience, after you've begun what I call the change or go process, you'll find that 80% of those who you start this process with will look for a different place to work and go on their own. It's easier to change work locations than it is to change behaviors, and at some level, conscience or subconscious, life-time non-team players know this. 10% will make the necessary adjustments. These are usually the employees who didn't realize their behavior was so distracting to the team. The final 10%, either because they can't or won't change, will have to be invited to work elsewhere. Do not feel too downhearted about having to work through a change or go process all the way to this point. If the employee is one who seemingly wants to do good work for the team but just can't fit into the system, then the most humane thing is to help them find a place that is a better match for them. If, on the other hand, you are working with an individual who is refusing to stop their non-team player behavior, even after its been identified repeatedly, then, again, its best they move on.

Remember, the goal here is to not suck as a manager. Without a doubt, one of the most commonly mentioned characteristics of managers who do suck is they don't take action when action should be taken to stop non-team player behavior. If I were to recommend just one of these five facts to follow, I would recommend this one most of the time. A non-team player's impact on a team is too detrimental to ignore. I promise all managers everywhere if they are consistent about minding even just this one fact, they will have happier employees.

The Suckometer and Taking Action

Behaviors:

- Manager pays no head to team members who speak of coworkers who are not working.
- Manager doesn't care if there is 'fighting amongst the troops' - thinks it keeps team members sharp.
- Manager lets bad behaviors of favored employees go too far, seemingly playing favorites

Suckometer Reading: 100% suck

Behaviors:

- Manager listens to concerns, recognizes there may be a problem but the only suggestion they offer is, 'work it out amongst yourselves'
- Manager recognizes there are issues but addresses them only jokingly in team meetings, never specifically addressing anyone about the matter
- Manager puts together a team agreement but doesn't follow up with others about it

Suckometer Reading: not great, not bad 50% suck

Behaviors:

- Manager leads team members in creating a team agreement and then takes consistent action to help team members follow it.
- Manager has conversations with team members as soon as non-team player behaviors occurs
- Manager openly encourages everyone to have caring, productive relations in the workplace.

Suckometer Reading: 0% Suck – A true leader!

Self Check
Where do you see yourself on the Suckometer for taking action? Rate yourself on a scale of 0 to 10. 0 is you could give a seminar on the topic. 10 is no way should you be a manager. (High scores on a Suckometer – not good.)

Suckometer Reading for Taking Action: _____

Action Plan for Taking Action
Regardless of your self-assessment score, consider ways to improve in this skill and put these ideas into practice. Use the following space to write your action plans for improving skills in taking action.

_____
_____
_____
_____
_____
_____

FACT 5: MANAGERS WHO COMMUNICATE THE NEED FOR SMALL ADJUSTMENTS AT WORK DON'T SUCK

Have you ever worked for someone thinking everything was fine, but then you find out by surprise, usually in a midyear or annual review, that all is not okay? How's that worked out for you? My guess is you weren't too wild about it. This is exactly why you need to share information about adjustments that are needed with the people who report to you. Share information, that is, unless you want to suck as a manager. If that's the case then just keep important information to yourself.

> *My manager, Sara, is generally an okay boss. She's upbeat, pleasant, and appreciative. But one thing she's not, is a good communicator – at least when it comes to sharing information about little but important things that can help us out on the team.*

I'm in charge of weekly reports for our office. I've had the task for a few months now. As far as I knew everything was going okay. Last week I was corrected on that assumption. It seems one line of the report wasn't being calculated correctly. There was a small error in one of the formulas in the spreadsheet.

At my review Sara said, "I would have loved to have given you a five but this small error not corrected week after week has become a big error and the people upstairs are upset about it. Sorry."

Sorry? Yes, me too. Like I said, generally, Sara is okay, but I'm not the first to be burned by this sort of thing. It's stupid. We're professionals. I'm pretty sure most of us can handle information about us doing our work better. Surprises are okay at birthdays and the holidays, but like this? Not cool. Not cool at all. It had an effect on my pay and promotion, and especially my faith in Sara.

John / Denver

People need to know where they stand. It gives them the foundation they need to succeed. Here's what I tell people in my on-site seminars. I like exactly what John had to say about this. Surprises are great for the holidays or birthdays, but they really suck if it's not a good surprise. Especially if it's a surprised delivered during an annual or semiannual review meeting. If you've ever had that experience, you know exactly what I mean. You didn't or wouldn't appreciate it as an employee so, if you don't want to suck as a manager, you won't do this to one of your team members.

If they are doing a great job, tell them. This was covered in the discussion of Fact 1. If they're not doing a great job, tell them. If they are doing fine except for needing to adjust in one area, TELL them. If it helps, think of this point as something similar to the Take Action behavior, but in this case the only action we're talking about is making sure your team members know the score in all things, both good and bad, about where they stand.

I find that sometimes it is that people don't take action because they don't have a strategy for the action they want to take. People in management positions are no different. They know they should do something, but don't know how to proceed. When it comes to sharing information that may not be pleasant to hear in the workplace, here's a strategy that I like. It's not original with me. Trainers, HR specialists and counselors have been using it for ages. I've heard it referred to as the sandwich method and it goes something like this.

Sentence 1 - Share a genuine compliment with the team member. By this I don't mean saying this like, "nice tie" or "I just loved those cookies you brought in last week." Nice try but not what's needed. I mean a genuine compliment about their work. For example, "Tom, I want to thank you for the great example you set with your promptness in opening the office every day." Consider this the first slice of bread on the sandwich you're making.

Sentence 2 - Share information about whatever needs adjusted. For example, "Tom, I want to thank you for the great example you set with your promptness in opening the office every day. You do a great job with that. One thing that will help the office out even more is if, just before the doors are opened every day, you remember to call the home office to ensure they know things are okay at our branch."

This second sentence is the meat of the sandwich you are making (or peanut butter and jelly, or turkey, or whatever middle stuff you prefer). Be specific about the adjustment that needs to be made. Whatever you do, do not start this second with the word 'but'. Essentially, the word 'but' is a verbal eraser. Whatever you said in your first sentence would be completely wiped out if this second sentence starts with the word 'but.' Think back for a moment about any time when you've heard those words coming at you. "I'd like to give you the raise but...", I really wish I could find more work for you here but..." You get the picture. To sum it up, there are two points to remember with sentence 2, be specific, and do not start with the word 'but.'

Sentence 3 – Provide a genuine statement of encouragement and support for the adjustment that needs to be made. You know your team member can do it, and you know that once this adjustment is made they'll be right on track again. For example, "I know you can make this small adjustment, add it to your pre-opening checklist and I'm sure it'll happen every day. I also know that with this one small change, we'll have our start up procedures exactly as they need to be." This is the second slice of bread for the sandwich. Like any sandwich, it's not complete without this second slice, so don't forget to add it.

As with any productive exchange, it has to be two-way. So you add a side to your sandwich plate with the very important, 'Are there any questions?'

In asking this, be ready for whatever feedback comes your way. If you have an open, honest, relationship, whatever concerns your team member has about the adjustment, will come out and the two of you can work through it. If you don't have the best of working relationships own up to it and work towards a better one. Obviously, the more interpersonal work you do on the front end, the smoother things will go when times like this arise. See Fact 1 for a refresher on this topic.

If having a simple conversation about adjustments that need to be made seems too difficult for you, then maybe you shouldn't be a manager. I believe though, if you have worked through the first four facts, and you are able to apply them in the workplace, then applying this fifth fact in the workplace should be easiest of all. The most important thing here is that you follow it. Fact 5 may not seem as difficult, or urgent as the others, but not tending to it can have equally damaging results. Think loss of trust, less effective work teams, less empowered team members, stuff like that. In short, team members need to know where they stand at all times. Managers who acknowledge this and act accordingly, don't suck.

The Suckometer and Communicating

Behaviors

- Doesn't see things that should be brought up with employees. Doesn't care when issues with employees do arise
- Knows there are a few things that should be changed about the way an employee is doing things but doesn't bring it up, ever

Suckometer Reading: 100% suck

Behaviors:

- Gives 'suggestions' or hints for doing the job differently. If employees are good at reading between the lines, they'll get what the boss really wants. If not good at this, they stay uninformed
- Gets around to telling employees what should be changed, but only after a lot of time has passed; sometimes too much time

Suckometer Reading: not bad, not great. 50% suck

Behaviors

- Sees issues that should be corrected and addresses them
- Talks to team members in a timely manner about adjustments that should be made.

Suckomenter Reading: 0% Suck – A real communicator !

Self Check

Where do you see yourself on the Suckometer for communicating when adjustments are needed? More importantly, where do you think your team members would rate you in this behavior? Are you brave enough to ask? Rate on a scale of 1 to 10. 10 = no way should you be a manager. 0 = you could write a book on the topic.

Suckometer Reading for Communication: _____

Action Plan for You in Communicating

If you have some work to do in this area, what work will you do? Consider ways to improve in this skill and put these ways into practice. Use the following space to write down your action plan for improving communication.

_____
_____
_____
_____
_____
_____ _____

SUMMING IT ALL UP

The goal of this book has been to share five of the most common complaints about bad managers and to provide strategies for improving management practices in these areas. To review, the five facts about managers who don't suck are these:

1. Managers who treat team members as **people** don't suck.
2. Managers who are **aware** of their situation at multiple levels don't suck. Different levels of awareness include a) what's happening with team members, b) the opportunities for the team within the larger organizations, c) the status of the organization in the field.
3. Managers who practice **real** delegation don't suck.
4. Managers who **take** action to stop non-team player behavior don't suck.

5. Managers who communicate early when small adjustments are necessary don't suck. So if you are the manager, **you** communicate!

Take a moment now to look at the first letter of the words in bold face type in each of the five facts listed. To help you along, here they are: **P A R T Y**. Here it is, the acronym for you to remember. I have been in management positions and counseled with others who are in similar roles for over 20 years. I find, as do others, that when employees have managers who apply all five facts discussed here, the responsibilities of a manager can actually be somewhat like a party. Fun, enjoyable, refreshing. Respect employees and they will respect you. Look out for their interests, and they will look out for yours. Offer opportunities for growth through real delegation and they will rise to the challenge.

Take an active role in ensuring non-team player behavior is not allowed. This will create the undying gratitude of every other team member. Communicate the need for small adjustments in a timely, professional manner, and those who receive the information will appreciate it too. In the process you will create a more effective, efficient team.

You don't have to suck but if do, there are things that can be done to fix this. If you fix it, not only with the people who report to you benefit, but the entire organization will benefit also. I wish you all the best of as you pursue this great effort.

THREE DOORS

In my line of work I get to hear about the experiences of others in the workplace on a regular basis. Some people tell me stories of workplace victories. More people tell me about how frustrating their job is. Even more people tell me about how trapped they feel. If you feel trapped where you're at, I have something I want to share with you. I first learned of this in a psychology class during my undergraduate years and it has been invaluable to me ever since. Those that I have shared this with have also found it worth knowing. I believe you will find this of value also. I call it the Doctrine of the Three Doors and it goes like this.

In life, in any situation we find ourselves in, there are three doors we can take. There may be variations on the themes but in the end, all of the possibilities boil down to only three real options. We can ignore the situation and hope things change. We can work to make changes in the situation as best as we can or we can remove ourselves from the situation. Let's look at each of these in greater depth.

Door Number 1: The first door is the easiest one to discuss. In live presentations I usually set up this part of the presentation with a question. "If you're in a situation you don't like, and you do absolutely nothing to change the situation, what are the chances that the situation will change?" Again, what are the real chances change will occur if your only strategy is hope. Everyone knows the answer – a big fat zero percent chance. Oh maybe there's a small chance the one tormenting you at the office will move or die, or the promotion that you've been desiring for five years will *eventually* come to you. But how much of your life do you want to spend hoping for that change? Chances are you've already spent too many of your days in this frustrating situation. In my opinion it's time to consider a couple of other options.

Door Number 2: This option is to make changes in the situation as best as we can. Door Number 2 is a challenging one because there are two factors in play here, your actions and the other party's response to your actions. You have control over the first, but hear me now and believe me three weeks from yesterday, you have zero control over others. (Sometimes reality really sucks doesn't it.) So you do what you can. If you have a good relationship with those who are involved, you have some chance of realizing a change. If the relations aren't good, or the people you're working with don't have sufficient care for your situation, then the chances are not great.

Still, you do what you can. Have the conversation, negotiate for change, suggest new ways of doing things to make your situation more tenable. I can't guarantee you'll get the change you're looking for if you do this but again, what are the chances you'll get the change you're seeking if you don't try? Yup. You got it, zero. We can hope for better than that though. If you try, who knows, you just may succeed.

Door Number 3: The exit door. Remove yourself from the situation. If we're talking professionally, this means you find another job. The new job can be inside the organization or outside of the organization. It doesn't matter. The important thing is that the job is somewhere else. Get out from underneath the very sucky manager. Easier said than done, you say? Yes, I know, I get that a lot. So to be clear, I'm not saying any of these doors are easy to step through. In my experience (and probably yours too) Door Number 1 is the door most commonly taken. This may seem strange when you think about it but after further thought, there actually is some logic to it. Door Number 1 is most often taken because the reality is, no matter how sucky the known situation is, fear of the unknown often scares people even more. This is so much the case that even in bad personal situations people will not take either of the other two doors. But I digress, back to more about Door Number 3.

Door Number 3 is to remove yourself from the situation. Earlier I stated that professionally this could mean find another job, but actually, you don't need to find another job, you just need another source of income, right? If you don't need the money then you sure as heck do not need the grief of working under or around people who suck. Now back to if you do in fact need the income.

The fact is, no matter how much we all say we like our jobs, we wouldn't work if we didn't have to. Anyone who says otherwise probably would say they like cold toilet seats, too. But back to the point, if you had a different source of income, you wouldn't need a job, would you? This is the reality that Trump and Kiyosaki wanted people to understand when they wrote, Why We Want You to be Rich. If the only concern is having what we need to pay the bills, then it shouldn't matter if those funds come from a job, or a different source.

Why We Want You to be Rich is over 350 pages long. The first 300 pages of have a great deal of information relevant to financially smart living for any time. The last 60 pages or so provide three suggestions for non-job-related ways to generate income. The authors promote non-job related income because most jobs, most salaries, do not pay enough to become financially independent. The three methods for producing income outside of a job that were cited by Trump and Kiyosaki are:

1. Through real estate, which is no surprise coming from two gentleman who have made millions this way.

2. Through the development of a one's own business, based on new or uniquely different products or services.

3. Through leveraging a proven business model already in use by others such as a franchise or credible network marketing organization.

Again, to be clear. I am not saying that any of the Door Number 3 options are easy. Finding a new place to work or any of the options suggested by Trump and Kiyosaki are not easy things to do. What I am saying is the options do exist. Those who choose to stay where they are and complain about it must realize that they are staying in the sucky situation they have as a matter of choice. Maybe it's the benefits, maybe the proximity to home, the money, maybe they don't want to move to another area where a job could be more easily found. It could be any number of reasons but the bottom line is, as bad as a sucky manager may make it for a person (you maybe?) you are choosing to stay in the situation. People do this because in their heart and/or in their mind, there are more reasons for staying than for leaving.

If you do consider Door Number 3, I recommend you have something else in place before you go. There are many options. Don't think there aren't. Those who think they don't have any options are doomed to stay trapped in the situation they are in. Those who ask instead 'what other possibilities can I create for myself?' will give their minds a chance to find an answer to this more empowering question.

This final section is definitely a topic for a completely different book but, at least here, I wanted to give you some food for thought. If you find yourself reporting to a manager who sucks, you have options. Consider them all, make a mindful decision, and then do whatever seems best. As long as you are making your choice deliberately, you'll be ok. You drive your own life, don't be driven by it.

NOTE TAKING SECTION

Use this section to track your goals, actions and results.

_____

_____

_____

_____

_____

_____

_____

_____

_____

_____

_____

_____

_____

_____

_____

_____

_____
_____
_____
_____
_____
_____
_____
_____
_____
_____
_____
_____
_____
_____
_____
_____
_____
_____
_____
_____
_____
_____
_____
_____
_____
_____
_____

ABOUT THE AUTHOR

Arron Grow is an organizational development specialist with more than 20 years of experience in the field. His experience in the workplace includes many years overseeing for-profit operations on college campuses, service as a Training and Support Team member and as an International Program Manager for MSN, Microsoft and the first Organizational Development and Continuous Learning Manager on the West Coast for Green Mountain Coffee Roasters.

Author, Presenter, and Producer, Dr. Grow, adds value to others by learning about, developing, and presenting information on topics of professional and personal development. His Ph.D. is in Educational Leadership with an emphasis in Adult Education and Training. He enjoys life with his wife and their children in Tacoma, Washington.

To contact Dr. Grow about this work or other topics related to his efforts in Workplace Sanity education, send an email message to info@workplacesanity.com.

ADDITIONAL WORKS BY THE AUTHOR

Audio Seminars and Books Available at www.apgrow.com

How to Not Suck as a Manager

Change or Go:
How to Stop Non-Team Player Behavior in the Workplace

You Know You Want It, Here's How to Get It: Lessons learned from
my years as Executive Producer and Host of Personal Best Radio

Archived Episodes of Personal Best Radio Available at:

http://archive.org/details/personalbestradio

AP Grow

KEYNOTE SPEAKING

To arrange a Workplace Sanity keynote with Dr. Grow for your organization, send an email message to info@workplacesanity.com.

Workplace Sanity Keynotes:

How to Not Suck as a Manager

Change or Go:
How to Stop Non-Team Player Behavior at Work

Stop Pretending You're Being Heard

You Know You Want It, Here's How to Get It